The Nobody

For Pat,

Everybody is a Somebody
because life is a miracle.

The Nobody

Garrett Buhl Robinson

Poet in the Park ®

In Humanity I see Grace, Beauty and Dignity.

Poet in the Park®
In Humanity I see Grace, Beauty and Dignity.
PoetinthePark.com

Contents

Some have said, "It's a dog eat dog world."
But I am not a dog nor do I want to eat one.

The Nobody

When everyone is quiet
    and nervous about everything,
in the heaviest silence –
    Nobody gets up to sing.

Everything is incomplete,
    the tasks run on and on,
there's no end to our errands –
    Nobody can get it all done.

All our demands are different
    as we answer our own call,
and from these diverse desires –
    Nobody can please them all.

When all is thought lost
    and life's a desperate climb,
no matter what the deficit –
    Nobody can come from behind.

Call this deluded hope,
    call my logic a crime,
but I know from experience –
    Nobody wins every time.

And in the most desperate hours
    of toiling endlessness,
stretch it out for eternity –
    Nobody has time for this.

You may weep for the loss of youth,
    always wish things were better,
you may dread growing old –
    Nobody lives forever.

Life's a terminal illness,
    everyone is doomed –
Nobody can survive.
    Nobody is immune.

Some call them nobodies,
   don't say you never hear it,
but if someone is a nobody
   then Nobody's all spirit.

And if nobody exists
   with no body to inflict
then I say this is a wonder –
   Nobody is perfect!

My day begins as it always has – with the opening of my eyes. My thoughts surface from the cool pool of slumberous sleep that had deepened through the night in the whirling currents of dreams. For a moment I enjoy the soft shades of early day pouring over the pavement. It is not until I begin to move that I feel the aches of another weary night where gravity mashed me flat on the ground. The traffic on the streets is relentless. All night, the wheels roll next to my head. Every time I drift to sleep, I wonder if I will wake. That makes every morning a gift, whether I want it or not.

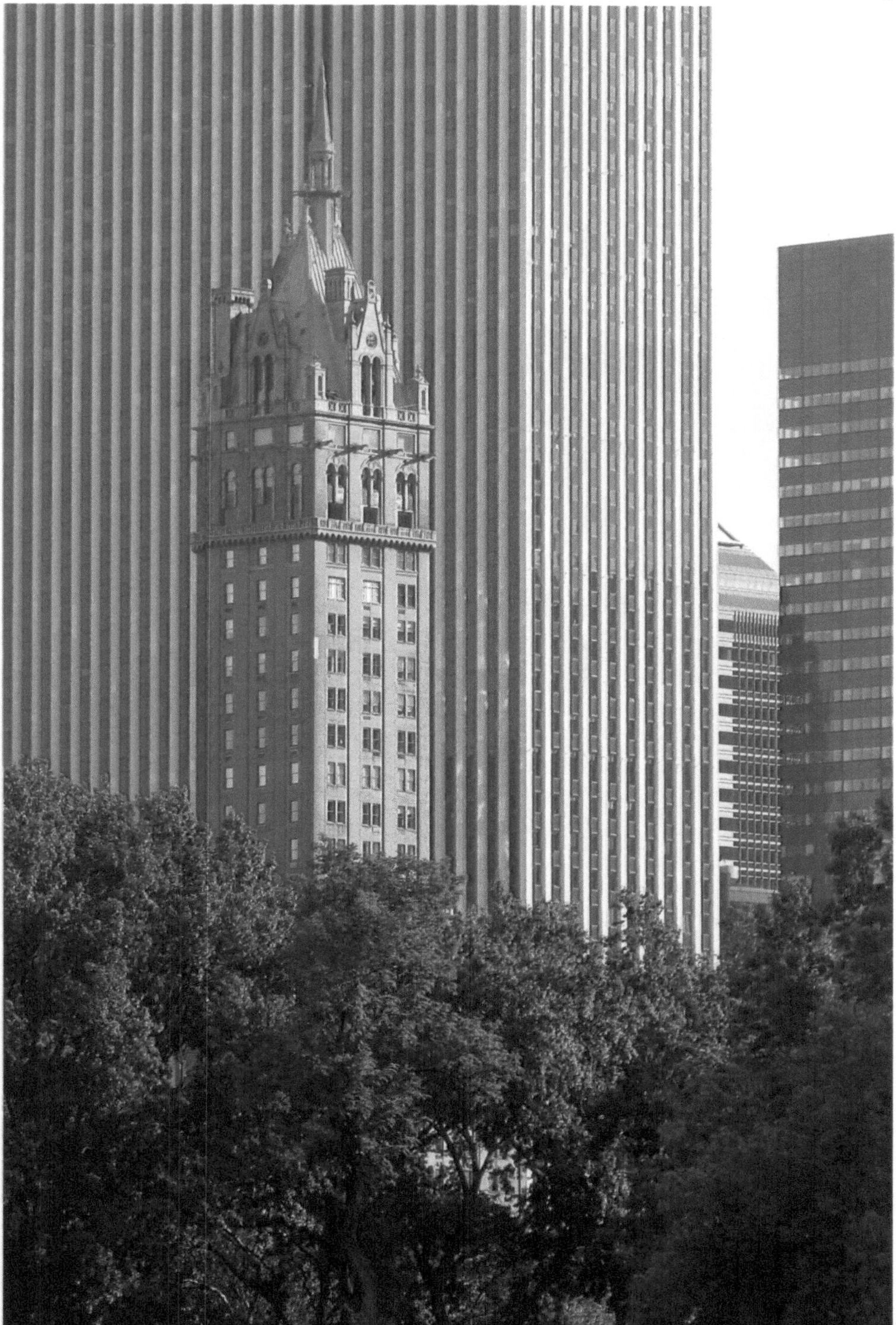

Places

They may call me a vagrant,
   say I've got no place to stay,
but every time I try to find a home
   people just drive me away.

They can call me trash,
   say nothing belongs to me,
that all I've got has been lost
   and I don't deserve a thing.

I might find a room
   to put my life in order
but the very next day
   my stuff's dumped on the street corner.

I'll gather what I can carry
   and continue on my way,
doing the best I can
   moving from place to place.

   And I've got a place at Central Park.
     I've got places with a view,
   places close to the subway,
     places on 5th Avenue.

   I'm surrounded by people.
     I'll never be alone.
   I've always got a place to stay,
     this whole city is my home.

I lug my stuff all over town,
    I don't even know what I have,
moving from place to place
    I keep my stuff in the bags.

You can kick me like a can,
    and call me a disgrace
but have you ever taken the time
    to look me in the face?

Of course once I'm dead
    I'll never live to see the day
but they'll probably dig me up
    and kick me out of my grave.

Maybe my casket will tumble,
    maybe my casket will roll
but I wouldn't be surprised
    if they kept kicking me from hole to hole.

Maybe they want some amusement,
    maybe it's something more drastic,
maybe they just want to hear my bones
    rattling in the casket.

But I've got a place at Central Park.
    I've got places with a view,
places close to the subway,
    places on Park Avenue.

I'm surrounded by people.
    I'll never be alone.
I've always got a place to stay,
    this whole city is my home.

A few years ago I quit my job and began selling my books on the streets of Manhattan. After spending nearly twenty years trying to reach publishers and literary agents, I decided to go directly to the public. With whom else do I aspire to speak anyway?

People often ask doubtfully, "Are your books self-published?"

I never hesitate to respond, "Yeah, just like Walt Whitman, William Blake, Virginia Woolf and countless others. I'm joining ranks with some of the greatest literary luminaries in the history of humanity."

Self-realization is not a defect. It's a distinction. I'm like Archimedes. With my little book stand, I will move the world.

I meet people from all over too. Every day in New York City, I can see the entire world through the wonder of each unique individual.

The World Comes to Me

When I think of the world
    and the breadth of diversity,
I think of all the wonders
    a travelling person can see.

But without the time
    and certainly lacking the means
I feel my only adventures
    are what I have in my dreams.

But I found a solution,
    it's more than a remedy
I moved to New York City
    and let the world come to me.

Every single person I meet
    brings insight from their life.
It's like I can see their world
    reflected on their eyes.

They bring their languages,
    they're traditions too,
and the different perspectives
    broaden everyone's view.

I feel their home's terrain
through their character's shape.
I know universal kindness
through their individual grace.

I get a sense of their climate
from their temperament.
I can sample their cuisine
from the taste of their interest.

But the greatest diversity
is individuality
and I encounter these wonders
in every personality.

I'm on this curb every day. While the thronging masses are passing, I keep asking if anyone wants to hear a poem. Then on some very rare occasions someone steps out of the shuffling crowd, walks directly up to me and says, "Yes." Then I just open my life and let all the poetry pour forth from me.

A Stage on Broadway

Vendors are cooking at every corner.
The stores are filled with silk and satin.
How could anyone call me poor
if I can afford to stroll through Manhattan?

I can wander forever on these streets,
the parks are filled with trees and flowers
and the moon's not too far out of reach
when I see it touched by the tips of these towers.

I'm at Times Square most every night,
the library has every book I can read,
and although I may not reach Rockefeller Heights
you can hear me performing on the streets.

I don't have a billboard or an agent
and I'm far from being a millionaire,
but they say "Location! Location!"
so I put my sign up in Times Square.

I'm out on 43rd most every day,
every moment of my life is show time.
I've got a stage right on Broadway,
I put my little stand up beneath the street sign.

Of course, most people ignore me, but that's their prerogative. I stay out of everyone's way. This is New York City. The pace is relentless. If you pause here, you can be trampled because this mass keeps moving and the momentum is merciless.

My question doesn't impose upon anyone. I'm certainly not an obstruction. By no means do I make anyone feel obligated to stop. I simply extend an invitation. I stand at a door that opens into dimensions of the imagination. It is a musical passage traversing our differences.

In the city, we are so close, yet we are so distant. We live in a world of strangers. I am simply extending a tiny thread over the chasms between us. If someone decides to pinch that frayed thread with their interest, the string may be tightened and tuned between us. It may be played like a musical instrument. That little line is a contact. Upon it bridges may be built as our overarching interests lean together to touch at the keystone of understanding.

World of Strangers

We often rub together,
    yet remain far apart,
our obstructions are close,
    yet our goals are afar.

We live in a world of strangers
    that remain removed
and in a world of strangers
    we become strangers too.

There are chasms between us
    and we reach out from the edge
but our empty embraces
    send us toppling over the ledge.

We may call out for others
    but our desperate cries
are lost in the commotion
    of the traffic rushing by.

There is the confusion of the crowd,
    the whole place is an uproar
but don't lose yourself in dissonance
    and believe it's only noise.

The city is a symphony
    of fluent melodies,
a vast orchestral movement
    through avenues and streets.

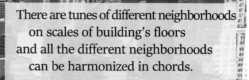

There are tunes of different neighborhoods
   on scales of building's floors
and all the different neighborhoods
   can be harmonized in chords.

The dimensions are colossal
   and the city is a machine
but when we start to feel the rhythm
   we can hear the city sing.

Every corner has a tone
   at every time of day,
take note of all the people
   in the arrangements they all play.

The conductors are in trains,
   the taxies blow the horns,
we all have our own instruments,
   we are all part of the score.

In our intersecting lives
   over-arching all the noise
when we start to hear the music
   we begin to find our voice.

When I do get a chance to talk with people, I generally have wonderful experiences. However there are occasional challenges. There was one instance when I was talking with a lady. I gave her my elevator pitch for a brief description of my books while also demonstrating my ability to articulate my thoughts. Then I began to recite her a poem. When I was midway through the poem, some guy walked up and began ranting something absurd. Then he punctuated his defamatory remarks by kicking my stand. All my books went flying in the air and tumbled onto the streets. I never stalled or stammered though. I kept reciting my poem without pausing or wavering from a single line while I reached down to pick up my books from the ground and set them back on my stand. When I had set everything back into place and finished my poem, I looked up at the lady and noticed she was crying. It was a heartbreaking sight. With what consoling comfort poetry may offer, I assured her no hostility would keep me from my work and there is a place of beauty where everyone can be safe.

Beauty

In the biggest city
    they may say I'll never be
but how can the biggest city
    not have any space for me?
I've got a place in my head
    where I'll always be free
and all I see
    is beauty.

Frost said the aim is song
    and I've never known Frost to be wrong,
and if you listen carefully
    in the engine blocks of this machine
breezing through the cacophony
    you may hear me softly sing
and all I sing
    is beauty.

Some say inside this factory
    you're either the teeth of the gears
or the fuel that's burning
    but with the pistons firing
and the boilers blowing steam
    you can hear me whistling
and all I whistle
    is beauty.

In all this boisterous noise
    there is no relief
and any chance to be heard
    is beyond belief
but when I have something to say
    you'll hear me speak
and all I speak
    is beauty.

Some say I'll never make it
    and I can't stand the heat.
Some say I can't do it
    and I'm going to get beat
and they'll pound me to smithereens
    till I'm a bloody pulp of dead meat
but even when I bleed
    I bleed beauty.

The few times I get harassed, I know I'm not being belittled. I won't allow myself to be belittled. I'm not going to fight though, I just keep developing myself. Those people aren't diminishing me, they're only diminishing themselves. Certainly some guy standing out on the sidewalk and singing isn't a threat. I just want to fill the streets with poetry. I'm just wringing out my tiny life to drip the sweetness of music into the roaring rush of this relentless river.

Diminishing Opinions

While they're waiting for me
    to fall behind
I'll be racing forward,
    bounding in my strides.

Diminishing opinions
    don't cause any damage.
Underestimations of me
    give me an advantage.

When people sit around
    slandering everyone else,
they're holding themselves back
    and belittling themselves.

People may pick a side
    but it's all the same
and I'm not playing
    and this ain't a game.

Some may get a lift
    when they see other's lose,
but they're on a see-saw
    that'll just drop them too.

I'd rather venture out
    and develop my own life
then I'm always winning
    as long as I survive.

Some may be content
    to dwell on what's well known,
I'll leap into uncertainty
    and see how far I can go.

Most of the people on the streets suffer terribly though. They live tortured lives. Of course they are tortured by the misery of their conditions and the humiliation of their circumstances, but most often, they are tortured by their own minds. When your own mind is the enemy, there is no escape.

Reality is indistinguishable from the imagination. One can't discern whether things are as they seem, or if everything is a treacherous deception. Every random statement can be twisted into slander. Every scuff of a passing step can be a disdainful dismissal. Even the pneumatic release of the brakes of the buses is an affronting derision. It is like living naked in a forest of thorns.

Other times, the search for purpose is endless. There is one guy I have seen around town who walks up and down the streets. I've never seen him sit. He may even sleep while he walks, like the whales in the sea swimming through their dreams.

As his shoes wore with use, he covered the holes with tape. As he added layer after layer, his shoes grew into big moon boots of duct tape permanently stuck to his feet. Day and night he wanders through the city. The only destination is exhaustion. The only peace is oblivious sleep.

Searching for a Purpose

We're all searching for a purpose
   to engage ourselves,
a fulfilling involvement
   with something else.

We're all stuck with ourselves
   our entire life,
to reach out for something else
   is an instinctive drive.

We are searching for affirmation
   that we exist.
We find meaning in life
   through our accomplishments.

For the acquisition of things
   some labor every day,
as if without all these things
   they would fade away.

Some consider their own lives
   not from what they obtain,
but make themselves feel better
   by soothing other's pain.

Parents can live through their children,
   their progeny,
then span time and space
   through their families.

We may look to our ancestry
   to see where we come from
and derive an identity
   from our origin,

but all these directions of attention
   can't go one way,
we must support one another
   with our various trades.

In our search for destinations
   where our urges are appeased,
we hope for validation
   in what we give and receive.

If we are affirmed by others,
   it's easy to tell,
when we help each other,
   we also help ourselves.

And if you consider this selfish
   I have only one reply –
we all share the same life
   like we share the same time.

I know some of the most fascinating people too. One of my buddies, Walt, is an opera fanatic. He said he used to hustle tickets in front of the Lincoln Center decades ago. One night he got stuck with an expensive ticket to the Metropolitan Opera and decided to see the show. He said it was the most magnificent thing he has ever seen in his life. He's been going ever since. I saw him earlier today. He was sitting in the library reading a biography of Bizet.

We're All Oddities

We all have our oddities
and peculiar qualities
but how do they mesh
with what others expect?

These distinctive qualities
of our personalities
can often lead
to alienating misery.

Society demands we conform
and our qualities inborn
can often make us targets
of ridicule and scorn.

What makes us unique
can make us feel like freaks,
but what sets us apart
can be our greatest strengths.

If we learn to protect
what others consider defects
we may work our little quirks
so they distinguish and impress.

The grandeur of royalty
is a type of eccentricity.
Within each one of us
is our own nobility.

I'm out year round too. I even set up my stand in the snow. Last year after one of the storms, I made up a snow person. Then *voilà*, I had my own captive audience.

Can you imagine a colder reception though? After every poem I would look up and he would just stand and stare with his frozen face and icy eyes. Still, I persevered and I read him poetry until he melted.

Meet the
Author

Garrett Buhl Robinson

Ways We Communicate

People may say what they want.
They may say what they do.
They may call me a loser.
They may call me a fool.

We all struggle at times
no matter what you believe.
Whether you're rich or poor
life is fraught with difficulties.

There are social circles
and the hoops of profession
but how we live our lives
is our greatest expression.

And of the countless ways
of communication
my aim is for beauty
and inspiration.

I live my life as it flows
and not by security,
my lines do not enclose,
they extend out radially.

The measure of my mind
is the wonder of its growth
not the narrow restrictions
of what I already know.

And if anyone asks
I will take it to task
and declare I am a poet
but not in what I say,
but through what I compose
and the music I make.

I've had some astounding reactions too. Some people have actually told me that I was the highlight of their trip to New York City. This always amazes me. Here, we are surrounded by museums filled with cultural treasures. The New York Public Library is one of the most important repositories of literary archives in the history of human civilization. This city is the dance capital of the world and the concert halls are overflowing with enchanting and rapturous music. The buildings towering around us reach the zenith of architectural achievement. Yet, surrounded by these marvels, I am always astonished when people stop at my wobbly bookstand to read my humble expressions and listen to little ole me sing. Even with all the magnificent monuments carved from immortal marble, people still seek the warmth of the human touch.

Make It Shine

Everybody starts out
  raw hide,
and what I've got,
  I'll make it shine.

Appoint the hour,
  I'll be right on time,
show me what you've got,
  I'll respond in kind.
People have their own,
  let them choose a side,
but I'm all over town
  and I'm living right.

I've got my books for sale
  and I can sing in key.
Living is tough
  but inspiration's free.
We never know what to expect,
  that's the wonder of the world,
but something good always comes
  from hard, honest work.

I've got my own business,
  I'm here day and night
and I'm in the business
  of sharing delight.
We'll never have a glut
  of inspiring beauty
and the world can never have
  too much poetry.

I ain't got much
  but what I've got is mine.
You can mint your coins.
  I'll make my dime.
From the tips of my shoes
  to the top of my mind,
what I've got
  I'll make it shine.

Yeah, I get critics too. Some people see no value in what I do. What's odd, instead of just ignoring me, they have to walk up and complain. Don't they have anything better to do? So I just keep singing till they smile.

What Succeeds

People may wonder
    why I live in misery
And why I can't apply myself
    more productively,
after all there are plenty
    of opportunities
to live my life
    more profitably.

But I'd rather maintain
    my moral integrity
from which I derive
    my sense of dignity.
I know the world
    and I own my deeds
and I would rather fail
    when I see what succeeds.

I'm not living a fantasy,
    I'm fulfilling a dream
and from what I sing
    I have my own means.
People may complain
    but I'm no bother.
Who really supports one's self
    when we depend on each other?

The people are passing
  endlessly
I can see them all
  from the soles of their feet.
They rush and stampede
  but they won't trample me.
I'm like a rock in the river
  while they run to the sea.

I live in the open
  where everyone can see.
Why should I be ashamed?
  I'm not hiding.
You come out for your job,
  you come out to the store,
what you need is outside
  and you'll always need more.

A bear may spend the winter
  hibernating
but even a bear must come out
  eventually.
No one can stay inside
  indefinitely,
at least not until
  they're in the cemetery.

Everything is here.
Some people go to the movies.
Some people watch TV.
Me? — I live in New York City.

Not Seen on TV

All I have are my poems
   you are welcome to read
and if you like
   you can listen to me sing.

But if you are wondering
   I can tell you one thing
what you see me perform
   you won't find on TV.

The television shows us what to watch,
   commentators tell us what to think,
advertisers lead us on
   and tell us what to eat and drink.

We have endless programs
   to confirm our beliefs.
We've got pharmaceuticals
   to numb our nerves for relief.

Can we deny what we see
   and believe everything we're told
or will we only listen
   to what we already know?

They'll build up the bad
   till they offend the whole town,
then they'll sell the tickets
   to watch them tear it down.

I don't need to change what I feel,
   no one shows me what to see.
I don't need a filter or a feed.
   The whole world's right in front of me.

So take a minute to stop,
   and please your curiosity,
I'll touch your life with music
   lilting tenderly.

Now I realize that out on the street I am a complete stranger to everyone. I don't have a stellar literary reputation to vouch for the quality of my work. I don't have laudatory diplomas framed on a wall behind me. I'm standing in between a street lamp and a garbage can. People open these books and they only see blots of ink on the page. I am the one who has to bring my work to life.

Still, even the best literature and art can't excite everyone. Sometimes it seems like people are only looking for ways to reject everything. There are plenty of times when I have told people that I can please anyone. And you know what they did? They just stood there and laughed at me. Then I said, "See, I knew you'd love my comedy."

Nothing They Like

All some people care about
   is what is wrong,
give them a place in the world,
   they'll say they feel alone.
In fact, give them anything
   and you'll be denied,
it's like they're only satisfied
   with what they don't like.

Show them wonders of culture,
   beauty polished pure,
they'll say it's too fragile
   and will never endure.
Take them to museums
   to see ingenious artistry.
They'll say all the paintings
   should be more like photography.

Give them a mountain,
   they'll complain about a mite.
Give them the sun,
   they'll say it's too bright.
Give them the moon,
   they'll say its fickle and plain.
Give them anything,
   they'll say they'd rather complain.

Show them the countryside
   and places without bounds,
they'll think you're trying
   to get them out of town.
Take them to the circus,
   they'll just sit and frown,
then accuse you for making them
   feel like clowns.

They'll say you're holding back,
   when you give them a hand.
Offer them a seat,
   they'll say they'd rather stand.
Even the tiniest error,
   they'll always detect,
make a simple mistake,
   they'll say you're life's a wreck.

Give them a compliment,
   they'll suspect a trick.
Wish them good health,
   they'll say you make them feel sick.
Give them something beautiful,
   they'll say it's not that attractive.
Give them a million of dollars,
   they'll complain about taxes.

Give them what they asked for,
    they'll certainly refuse.
Give them one of a kind,
    they'll insist on having two.
Whatever you offer
    it will never be right.
Give them everything,
    they'll say there's nothing they like.

Of course some people ask me when I work. They say I'm always sitting outside and wonder when I get anything done. Really, it's not a matter of when I work. The question is: When don't I work? In the morning I write, in the afternoon I recite, in the evening I read and when I sleep, I tinker with my dreams. Art is my life and my whole life is a work of art.

With the Lunatics and Lovers

I've been kicked to the curb
  but I'm hovering above the gutter.
You can call me what you want
  but you shouldn't even bother.
All that I can show you now
  you won't see from any other.
Watch me dancing in the streets
  with Shakespeare's lunatics and lovers.

Sometimes standing in the rain
  is the only way I have to bathe.
I've got a shower from the skies
  I'll be cleaned before your eyes,
and even living on the streets
  I still floss and brush my teeth.
I may have lost everything
  but I'll keep my dignity.

Let them cry about utility,
  I'll keep offering ingenuity.
They wonder what's around the curve
  but anything new they'll call absurd.
You can wager on what others prize
  but if they take your winnings don't be surprised.
They can rest their eyes on what they're shown
  but the biggest thing is the unknown.

They say I'll always be left out,
  but I'm too big to fit in.
They tell me to give it up,
  and I will as I ascend.
They say I'll always be on the streets
  but look at all the people I meet.
They say I've gone too far,
  but how else will I touch the stars.

I've been kicked to the curb
  but I'm hovering above the gutter.
You can call me what you want,
  but you shouldn't even bother.
All that I can show you now
  you won't see from any other,
watch me dancing in the streets
  with Shakespeare's lunatics and lovers.

I admit there were times I lost my way. I desperately sought how to share my love of literature with others. For one stretch, I aimlessly staggered through the streets. I would pick up pieces of paper trash and write rhyming couplets on them. Then I would let them go and watch them scuttle off in the wind, tumbling and crumbling until they eventually dissolved into the sea – my little inkling lines sinking into the darkening deep. I said if I couldn't speak with the people then I would write my script on oblivion.

Shelley and Keats

The songs turn sour,
    flitting in the moaning breeze,
a summer happiness
    extending beyond reach,
the sun is setting
    blighting all I see,
makes me weep
    for Shelley and Keats.

Driven boundless
    before the gusting scream,
flailed and tossed
    on tumultuous seas
and every wondrous discovery
    no one will believe,
makes me weep
    for Shelley and Keats.

Behind the shuttered panes
    of the battered lees,
the roiling clouds
    pouring and thundering
with howling winds
    splintering trees,
makes me weep
    for Shelley and Keats.

Can you hear Adonais
    beautifully sing?
And the most lovely music
    sadly fading?
All the herds are dropping
    to their knees,
makes me weep
    for Shelley and Keats.

When kind affection
    has no company,
when love is lashed
    and hate runs free,
they crown the crass
    and praise the thieves,
makes me weep
    for Shelley and Keats.

A couple of years ago a guy walked up to me and said, "You know, I don't believe it. You'll sit out here all day just to sell one book."

I told him, "You don't understand. It has taken me 20 years to sell this book. Waiting one day isn't too long."

I Do What I Do

There is no question why we wonder
about the motives of our lives
but people are often puzzled
when I say, "I write so I may write."

What I most desire is to spend my time
transcribing my thoughts at a desk
while contemplating a sense of life
and exploring ideas in my head.

I would rather be a pedestrian
on the streets of New York City
than circling the Mediterranean
in a racy car in the Grand Prix.

I would rather cook my modest meals
on a humble stove of my own
than engorge myself with a feast
in another's palatial home.

I would rather sit in peace and quiet
where I can concentrate and read,
than waltz through flashy nights
with champagne celebrities.

I shun a crowd of concubines
and make no claim to be a king.
I am a single, pauper poet
sleeping alone with the love of my dreams.

Of course, what I want means nothing
if my desire remains a fantasy.
Practice is the guide for my work
as I make my dreams a reality.

The way I see it, I may be lost but I'll keep moving through the mystery. On the stage of every day, I stand before the entire world with nothing more than a song, and I sing.

Garrett Buhl Robinson is originally from Trussville, Alabama. In 1992, he jumped on a coal train at a switchyard near his hometown and through the years he has been traveling around the United States while studying intensely, writing prolifically and supporting himself with odd jobs.

Without any success reaching publishers, he decided to self-publish his books and move to New York City in 2011.

He also adapted his novella, *Zoë*, into a solo musical which he performed at Off-Broadway venues.

If you're ever in Midtown Manhattan, listen beneath the sound of the rumbling machine that is New York City and you may hear him softly singing.